NOL ALEMBONG

The Passing Wind

(Poems)

MIRACLAIRE PUBLISHING
Kansas City (MO)

MIRACLAIRE PUBLISHING LLC
Kansas City, (MO) USA

Website: *www.miraclairepublishing.com*
Email: *info@miraclairepublishing.com*

ISBN-13: 978-0615895826
ISBN-10: 0615895824

Printed in the United States of America

"Unless the wind blows you do not see the fowl's rump"

– Igbo proverb

PREFACE

This revised edition of Nol Alembong's *The Passing Wind* has been enriched with four new poems making a total of thirty. The additions significantly buttress thematic content, form and style while inviting the reader to relish the intensity, originality and persuasive appeal of the creative world of one of Anglophone Cameroon's finest poets.

Grounded in the poet's historic-socio-political environment, the poetry is set against a backdrop of the oppression, violence, despair and misery characteristic of the postcolony. It constitutes a concrete social census of the ravages, both natural and human, of imperialism, autocratic leadership and sycophancy in the running of day to day affairs in postcolonial Africa. The poems enact the drama of existence in a context of diverse and often contradictory visions as we find in "Vision", "The Hamadryad," "The Game" and "Science and Life", among others. Here, as in other poems of this nature, symbolism, landscape images and invectives become purveyors of the poet's vision; a revolutionary vision rooted in endurance, unity and struggle, which begins firstly with obliterating certain inhibiting angles of vision. In "Facing the Odium," for instance, the reader is enjoined to "have this lens/Now that the mist has come to stay." The lens, as a symbol, effectively foregrounds the poet's desire to have his compatriots view the present dispensation clearly so that they can join forces together to bring about change, as we find in "Come, Brothers"

So,
Let us roll our God-given strength
And run up the anthill, for it must collapse
Under the lead that is our weight.

The power of art and that of the artist to bring about a new constellation is evident in this volume. Art is shown to be essential in diagnosing and solving today's repulsive social conditions. In this context, the poet, "the dog of the house", rallies his fellow brothers based on the belief that collective action can help transport people beyond negation to an affirmation of life.

The central motif on which the collection is built is the wind. As "nature's fizzle" the wind has both positive and negative effects on nature and man. It is the wind of change, in the title poem "The Passing Wind." In "The Way of the Wind" this "chameleon of the savannah" endows other natural elements with the ability to survive or gain an upper hand in a situation of uneven power relationships. In "Leeway," the last poem in the collection, it is against the backdrop of the wind that the poet-persona envisions a lush new world conceived in ecological terms wherein rain greens the fields, dead leaves give birth to corn and dead logs spit out mushrooms.

We are in the realm of written art in this collection but the overarching modes of thought and imagination shaping most of the poems is oral.

Alembong has a strong grasp of his people's oral culture; a grasp that informs his themes and styles. Whether he laments the loss of African values as in "The Christmas Chicken," investigates the perennial conflict between Christianity and indigenous religion as in "Changing Planes in Mid-Air" or examines apartheid as in "Steve Biko and His Fist", the poet employs verbal art forms such as call and response, proverbs, animal symbols and Nweh beliefs with remarkable originality and to good effect.

This revised edition of *The Passing Wind* is written in accessible style and lends itself to a multiplicity of interesting readings. In it the poet's diligence as a craftsman is foregrounded.

Eunice NGONGKUM (PhD)
University of Yaounde 1
Yaounde, Cameroon

Preface to the First Edition
1991

The Passing Wind presents the message of a Cameroonian to his fellow Africans and mankind in general. In the wide-ranging impressive collection, Nol Alembong dilates on the hierarchy of the physical and spiritual components of man, underlining in the process that purity and integrity are foremost among the values that man ought to uphold. Like some of his predecessors, the author occasionally assumes the role of a critic, alerting Africans about the danger which misuse of power and injustice pose to their development.

Although the author takes great delight in universal subjects, the core of his poetry relates to Africa, notably Africa torn between indigenous and foreign cultures and the drawbacks which the continent has suffered as a result of repressive systems of governance and unrealistic thinking. The poet's final note of optimism in poems as "Some Day for Sure", "The Last Ember" and the title poem, should however not be taken for granted. According to Nol Alembong, solace shall come to Africans not like manna from heaven but through cooperation, endurance, adequate planning and judicious dispensation of time.

In "Christmas Chicken", the author counsels Africans to return to traditional modes of worship if they are unable to practice imported religions correctly. In "The Gospel Singers", the author again contends that increasing religious fervour is not only distracting the people from genuinely struggling for survival, it is ironically not eliminating social ills as one would have expected.

The Passing Wind unfolds some of the potentials of a young poet, who is also a prospective novelist. The collection highlights a fertile and current mind, a humorous and impressive style and a perception giving due regard to African traditional beliefs and natural world. Nol Alembong has a strong predilection for African plants, insects and especially animals, whose members he parades with grace and felicity as in the following comment on apartheid:

> They say some are as white
> As the excrement of a sick fowl.
> They say some are as red
> As the anus of a gorilla.
> They say some have patches of skin
> Like that of the leopard.
> They say some change the look of their skin
> As the chameleon does.
> ("Steve Biko and His Fist")

Further in the same poem, Steve Biko's fence is described as follows in compounded similes for maximum effect:

> The top was covered with thorns of iron,
> Thorns as sharp as the teeth of a rat,
> Thorns as sharp as the prickles of a porcupine,
> Thorns as sharp as the claws of a hawk,
> Thorns as sharp as the beak of a vulture.

Nol Alembong's animals are palpable symbols correctly matched in the author's imagery. Thus, elements of repression are encapsulated in the heavy-weight elephant while the marvellous power of survival of the down-trodden masses is likened to the carapace of the tortoise.

The Passing Wind is a notable collection of poems written by a diligent craftsman. It is a significant contribution to existing literature in English and African poetry. I am indeed very proud to present this book to every student and lover of literature.

Professor Stella M.A. Johnson
University of Lagos
Lagos, Nigeria

Contents

Vision

The bat rises with the moon
And sleeps with the sun.
The eagle rises with the sun
And sleeps with the moon.

At midnight
The bat sees the ant's trail;
At noon
The eagle does not.

WIND

Wind,
Nature's fizzle,
Envelopes of steam
Floating kite-like,
Weaving the world
In a frantic dance.

Wind,
Wet, you soften the earth;
Wet, you green the fields;
Wet, you feed the world.

Wind,
Dry, you harden the earth;
Dry, you brown the fields;
Dry, you starve the world.

Wind,
At full blast, you weaken the earth;
At full blast, you uproot the fields;
At full blast, you flatten the world.

Wind,
What is in your barn
That makes you
The breadbasket of the world?

What is in your claws
That makes you
The hawk among fowls?

What is in your horns
That makes you
The buffalo among cattle?

Wind,
What is in you
That makes you
The chameleon of the savannah?

Chameleon of the savannah!
Greening the world you give it soul,
Browning it you give it hemlock.
The world stands, greening;
It falls, browning.

The Passing Wind

It came suddenly
And caught us, as if unawares.
It came limping
Like a child learning to walk.
It came naively
Like the chameleon in the race to immortality.

And we saw our soft lips
Turn to scabs.
We saw our tough soil
Crack to let microbes in.
We saw our trees
Shiver in their shoes.
We saw them
Drop their leaves in a falling sickness.
We saw our fowls
Lose their feathers to the chill.
We saw our animals
Abort their babies for lack of food.
We saw our rivers
Expose their stony ways
And our fishes preyed on by hawks.

And when we looked round
To see what was driving things mad
We saw that it was
The passing wind.

The Way of the Wind

The Passing wind
Gives sight to the bat
That fights the night
And blinds the sparrow
That accepts the night.

The passing wind
Gives sight to the mole
That burrows for shelter
And blinds the squirrel
That sleeps on trees.

The passing wind
Gives sight to the mother hen
That fights the hawk
And blinds the mother buffalo
That accepts the lion.

The passing wind
Gives sight to the eel
That opens the crocodile's mouth to see its teeth
And blinds the deer
That accepts the snake's bite.

The passing wind
Gives sight to the bug
That sucks to live, not to kill
And blinds the wasp
That stings to kill, not to live.

Come, Brothers

Come, brothers.
The dog of the house calls.
Come, stand on the anthill
And let the mound give way
Under your weight.

Leave this chosen vale of your lives:
This vale, this vale of tears.
Grope your way up the anthill
And let the mound give way
Under your weight.

The dale may be the rose of your lives,
But it's only the surface of the deep
And therein only the laughter of babies
May be heard: laughter in tears.

So,
Let us roll our God-given strength
And run up the anthill, for it must collapse
Under the lead that is our weight.

Did you say the queen ant
Will raise a stink?
But what does it matter if one is stunk
In the dust of the mound?

Facing the Odium

You may have this lens
Now that the mist has come to stay.
What is man if he can't see beyond his nose?
But put on the tortoise's shell
If you don't want the elephant to stop your breath.
Or will you continue with your gift of shades
When the darkness is swallowing you up?
You may as well ask the owl to pluck off its eyes.
Maybe you don't want a friend
To worry about you drowning –
I may as well tell a child
Not to mourn his mother's death.

The Hamadryad

Only drugged minds
saw any liniment
in the venomous spittle
emitted each minute
of coiling seasons
spent in the barbed-wire fence
that spelled the triangular boundaries
of the neonate empire where the
hamadryad reigned in awful command.

Maybe they didn't notice that
after each majestic hiss
walls of frogs were bugged
to whet the wolf's lust for flesh.

Didn't they see surgeons topping
diseased bodies on wonky tables?

Didn't they see piecing tentacles
spreading on rose beds
to harvest white petals?

Didn't they see the blind
teaching sharp eyes
how to read the hamadryad's bible?

Still,
some mortgaged the air we breathe
for a mosaic of fragile fragments;
and our skinny trunks

rolled with that of
the fat and greasy whale-like hamadryad
through twenty-five murky and stony ways.

And didn't the tortoise unveil
the dogmatics of hamadryadism?
Weren't the hallelujah cantors lined up
and made to stare at the mid-day sun
with their naked eyes?

But who can say
whether hamadryadism breeds lambs?

The Flower on the Mound

And it stood valiantly
as if that breath that ordered
things to take their various shapes –
at creation, that is –
went into its moulding alone.

And there it stood, the flower,
on the lonely mound a-field:
golden,
unruffled,
unrelenting,
like the Marine Corps Memorial
that stands on Columbian soil.

And beneath the clay lies the dust
that once was flesh – this flesh,
this decorated earth with which we go about,
this earth we go about with,
this with which we pride ourselves very much,
this flesh:
chubby,
frilled,
frail,
like chocolate ice cream in the face of the sun.

Still,
the flower on the mound blossoms
while the flesh beneath ever decays:
the two are locked in a room –
in the room of life and death.
The soul sprouts with the blossoming flower
while the flesh pays to the earth its slimy debt.

WAIT

Why do you make vain
To climb this baobab tree of ours?

True, the dog-nose coldness of the undergrowth
Is a passion hard to bear
But the compost is warmer
Than foliage isolated in mid air.

Sure, the rags over your nakedness,
The shades on your eyes,
The lock on your lips,
May spark your heart
To crimson readiness.

But why waste stones on birds
When the elephant hunt is yet to come?

Every dog has its day.

SCIENCE AND LIFE

We were told that
If X is the sufficient cause of Y
Whenever evidence of X occurs
There will be an occurrence of Y.

But when millions of mouths
Are said to feast on meatballs
In morphean paradise (as founded by Moses)
While one sees Kwashiorkor children
Comb earthen streets for juicy termites
The eye loses the glimmer of the half-blind
Upon examining the evidence of X.

THE CHRISTMAS CHICKEN

I caught hold of it –
The grip was firm.
The cock-a-doodle-doo
Was plaintive enough to let it go.

But the children were there –
The cry was a flint to float their joy.
They swallowed hard the meal
That was not yet a-cooking.

That pot was our yearly joy,
The joy that opened our eyes
To our naked ignorance –
The ignorance of Forsyth's forsythia.

For the man whose birth we celebrate
Washed down our sins with his blood
So too must we offer innocent blood
To welcome this great washer-man.

The message had been swallowed
With the greed of Tortoise in the sky
Unknown to him he was in a foreign land
With the birds' feathers stuck on him.

And so we folded our arms and closed our eyes
And swallowed this strange communion
Forgetting we could be stripped of our borrowed feathers
And abandoned in mid air.

Zombie

Always caught unawares
in the zizz that is his forte
and zipped up to the zodiac
of a mercurial brotherhood –
the brotherhood of a cat and a dog
licking the same boots,
the dry boots of a dog-eat-dog master –
as if his dead roots could send up more sap
to nourish that which is given up for lost.

For sure,
although the cat wails
all night in the den
the hour will come
when its keeper
will sing
his own
dirge.

MAY DAY

Yes,
that eagle-eyed manager
with blown-up jaws,
with rosy lops below
tough, trimmed moustache,
with bunion-like belly
on ostrich-like legs …

And
the tantalized serfs,
hazy about details
of the arrangement,
allow themselves to sink
into the pit of serenade
while the employee reigns
in a scarlet balcony.

Yet,
they love to hear their own ballads
catalogue the gains of battle,
to hear their coarse voices
shower gold dust on the master's head
for having opened their eyes
to the beauty of squalor.

THE GOSPEL SINGERS

Transcribed alleluias
placed on the tongue
on of a dried-throat cantor …

One, two, three, go!

And metallic voices
picked up the celebrated jingle
in mid air
apostrophizing
eulogizing
deifying
earth:

The eye of the blind: Yé!
The feelers of the numb: Yé !
The mouth of the dumbfounded: Yé!
The easel of human live: Yé!

And the sounds rippled
the surface of the wind
while corn decayed in the fields
with neglect.

The deity gone
(how short-lived the canonizing sermons!)
new cantatae now stick to the lips
of self-proclaimed griots …

One, two, three, go!

And the raucous voices
clashed in mid air
as they rattled along
validating
glorifying
sanctifying
ether:

An offspring on the stool: Hurray!
An umbrella over our heads: Hurray!
An icon for children of ghosts: Hurray!
An oasis in the desert: Hurray!

With speckled eyes riveted on the sun
and a riptide running rife
how can manna be a gain
or the boat be brought ashore?

EYE TO EYE

Like a man stares
at the naked sun
to discover the wires
that light its multiple bulbs
I planted my eyes on her face
to decipher the chameleon in her.

Eye to eye
one sees the dancer in her
as her eyelids juggle with her clients
the way naked groins maintain their balance
in the face of a rough night.

Eye to eye
tear ducts betray
the wetness of love
while the brown eyelids
throw dust in my eyes.

Eye to eye
the iris and the white
betray the hybrid in her:
the one showing the darkness of Eve,
the other the purity of Eden.

Eye to eye
you see the eyesore that they are:
their painted bodies are eyries
that breed serpentine habits
as worms keep falling into wet mouths.

Eye to eye
you see them with conjunctivitis,
they who can’t look at the sun
with the naked eye –
they must put on shades!

The Last Ember

From its socket
strolling
along the pavement of the wind
that Mind –
a silent storm in motion,
travelling,
an emissary in look
deigning not the deities –
that Mind
catches an ember in a dying fire:
an elm in ruin, once thought
an elixir for embalmed corpses
caught in their own corral !

And,
caught between green pastures
and the gobbling slaughter house,
this ember,
this neophyte,
stares at his own otiose oscillation
with the eye of the blind.

And,
in crimson readiness,
phoenix-like,
the coal consumes itself
with a denying ability.

May the phoenix never see half a millennium again!
May it never rise from its own ashes again!
May this be the last ember to gnaw our woods!

Some Day for Sure

Oh, how snake-like the trembling cry
Twines the small of my brains!
The feeble cords of that voice
Spell the agonies of the tortoise
Down trodden by the elephant.
But for how long will this last
When the tortoise's shell is hard to crack?
The journey may be too long and hard,
But was the chameleon not the first
To drum the long awaited message of death?
Where was Dog
Who thought the race was his?

The Tap Root

Oh, how sandy
The soil you explore!
How sandy, yet slippery it is!
How sensitive the touch of your hairs is
That you bore through the foggy darkness
Of man-made-earth unharmed?
Could it be your cap shading the hash light
That you would brave the rock on your path?
Perhaps the will to die for your straightness
Does make the thorns in the soil shut off.
Perhaps the joy in seeing things straight
Does dry up the venom in venomous curves.

Vain Hope

I dropped hooks
but baits anchored
on the edge of life and death
and the catch that I thought was mine
became a stubborn hope – for ever!

What water riddle
can play pranks
on a grey-hair fisherman?
The surface of the deep is rocky
but he knows the mossy parts of the bed
that should attract happy lovers.
Could it be that the fishes were so caught
in the web of love's greasy tentacles
that my hooks were seen as greenhorns?
Or that the whole surface shook
with my aging hands at the hook's end
that I couldn't notice the exact spot
of the love dance?
But who will first reveal to me
why an owl hard wailed on my roof
the night before the fish hunt?

Married Widows

Like a cock's crow
That reminds one
Of the break of yet another day
Their daily alleluia
Tore the garment of the night
And the cornea of the morning sky
With retrospective exhibitions:

The armoured-clad ship
That redirected the spears
Meant for spongy hearts!

The haloed head
That led the body
In misty weather!

The voice of reason
That told our story
When lurked in dumb show!

The Shakan soul
That, great and determined,
Led the people to victory!

But when the hooting owl
Whooped to announce the departure
Of the throwaway paper cup
That the monster was
And the purring cat
Grunted in the throat

In that house of pain
The wives were caught
Mid way their practised songs
And forced to wait –
How pusillanimously –
For the chosen son for the stool.

The stool occupied,
Frightened widows came
In a stooping stoogeology –
Still white with the funeral ash
Of their fallen husband.

And were they not caught
In the debacle of a greybeard
Taking the alphabet all over again?

THE GAME

The two teams ran in
Skipped and kicked the air
In the field of play
And the referee was there
And the whistle he had
In the field of play.

Our boys looked tough
For they ran here and there
In the field of play
But the others stood still
Only waiting for the whistle
In the field of play.

And the crowd was alive
As we ran here and there
In the field of play.
The blast of the whistle went
And the game took off
In the field of play.

I had my legs
And had the ball
In the field of play
And the referee was there
And the whistle he had
In the field of play.

I kicked the ball
And made a goal

In the field of play
But it was denied me
For the referee was there
In the field of play.

The rules were clear
And I kept to them
In the field of play.
But the referee was there
And the whistle he had
In the field of play.

The crowd cried loud
Calling him to order
In the field of play.
But the whistle he had
And the power he had
In the field of play.

The other team was there
And the team was his
In the field of play.
And the boys were lead
And their legs were slow
In the field of play.

The ball he gave them
For he feigned our fault
In the field of play.
And the penalty goal they had
The only goal a net had
In the field of play.

The crowd cried loud
And cursed and cursed
In the field of play.
But the whistle he had
And the power he had
In the field of play.

THE WAY

From the podium
The bleating voice
Taught the new creed:
How to be left-handed
In one's hastened dotage.

And doltish disciples
Picked up the doctrine
With blandished zeal,
Bleeping the alleluia
Of their blessed Christ.

And our eyes opened
To the wonder of all times –
Mohammed's men genuflecting
In unilateral single blessedness,
Caps on, mouths open, for the Eucharist!

And the lizard of the homestead
Passed for that of the farmland;
And the fowl passed for the partridge;
And blood passed for palm-wine;
And frightened owls hooted at noon
At seeing the way the world was going.

But this avowed axis,
This dum-dum all over the land,
This dreaming sickness
Of seeing dotards left-handed
Will surely wreck Abraham's yacht.

DENYING MELPOMENE

Who knows if one should hold fast to dreams,
Harbouring in his skull's roof
A red glow to thaw the heavy night,
Tending in cerebrum's nursery
Unsung lilies to unseat hawthorns,
He'd go flying like the eagle
Or sink like a beaten vessel?

Yes, there the whisper goes,
Running rife in a multitude
Of bulldozed psalmodists:
Should the myrtle lose its godhead
Because it must scratch the sky?

But had Eve refused to sink,
Guarding her unbitten nipples,
How would Eden and all its gem
Have grown from erect sensations?

Unless a grain lies beneath the clay
It remains an only grain.

And so the Jordan in one's head
Must flow with baptismal denial,
Thawing the fog between wolves and lambs.

MORES

Some time ago
Our queue produced a meteor
For our dark passage of life
And lo, mating cries deflated the rhythm
Of throbbing drums.

Now
The quip is that
Our tickets were not meant
To be exchanged for the light we craved for
But to buy glue for the dividing lines in the ant-hill
Left by invading soldier-ants.

And
Silent voices of brandishing guns
Deafen our cry to see the light
And sullen looks dyke us away from our creed
While ears are pinned to lamp-posts
To pick up unspoken thoughts.

And daily
Flowing ink plucks us
From our vantage points.

But
It is only when an egg drops
That a messy secret is revealed.

TO KEVIN

Son, to your own dictates must you listen.
Listen to the rumble in your inside
And the whistle from without do not heed
For it does lull the mind to sleep.

And whenever you do chance to speak
The tongue of your conscience must you speak.
Do not bite your lips for want of words
That dwell not in your mind's wards.

Speak your heart's lofty desire
For that will make you a fire
Not what into your ears is blown
For that will make you a drone.

For in ancient ages, as our sages hold,
Lived a folk's daughter, fair to behold,
Wedded to an elf, scorning her kind,
But just a head was he, dismayed to find.

And it flowed

(Tribute to B.B.)

Alas!
The labourer burrowed the soil –
How dry its every pore! –
To reach tap-root's end
For a drop for thirsty throats.

And at dead end prophetic voices
Announced the sap flow:
And Palm-Wine Will Flow!

Niched mummies watched with parting lips
The corporal discharge of pandemic pantomime.

And it flowed with vaginal denial
To unseat the embryonic glibness
Embossed with soppy glaze – ah ah!

And it flowed, cleansing Mandela's earth
The way rainstorms harvest nauseous dust
From our weeny streets of naked earth.

And it flowed to unleash the Nixons
From the splendour of Watergate Palaces
To the slimy gutters of Soweto.

And it flowed, and swept miasma to Hades,
And the testimony became our hagiology –
Ah, a red feather for the neophyte!

THE EARTH SPIDER

(For Bernard Fonlon)

Like the baobab tree
that shakes hands with both
the sober strife and frantic calmness
that spell the frontiers of man-made earth
is felled by some fateful knife,
thou, O Muse,
a satellite surged up
from the pool of calm waters
to the boil of crescent skies
art floored by ever looming winds.

How low the Tower lies!
(How disquieting Eiffel may lie!)
Why, O Lord, or whoever,
must sequin lie beneath the clay?

Alas the hour
when the Scribe's nib ceased to flow!
The fountain is dry, a herald's voice seems to say.
But in store serene serums
are littered for bottomless posterity.

What in man is loftier
than the littleness you always sought to be?
What manner of man is he
that, when cathedral heights
are the longings of fire-hot throats,
would seek to conquer the depth
of sequestered parishes?

Could it be this that made you
the Eiffel now lowered?
Could it be this that made you
the Earth Spider?

Changing Planes in Mid-Air
(To the memory of Okot p'Bitek)

I

The mother
Who they say is my aunt,
The sister of my mother,
Calls me pagan.
She calls me the uncircumcised
As if she didn't eat palm oil
At the ritual when my manhood
Was exposed to elders and age mates alike
And its foreskin cut off
To let blood wet the earth
The blood
That quenched the thirst of our ancestors.

She says
Big book has ruined me
Like faggots that have been eaten up by termites.
She says
I don't go to church,
The Whiteman's house of worship,
Because my books teach me strange things,
Things that make me turn my back to the God
Who they say lives in the sky;
Things that make me follow the black path
Said to lead to Satan's chiefdom;
Things that shall make me feast on fire
In the country of wizards.
When I try to picture this mother of mine –
This black skin with white blood –

Sleep finishes in my head.

II

This mother
Who they say is my younger sister
Is now the White God's child –
The White God who lives in a country in the sky.
And she says
I am the child of the Black God –
The Black God who lives in rocks
And in streams,
And in baobab trees.
She says
Her God is the true God
For He is the God of Abraham
And of Isaac
And of David.
She says
My God is the God of my fathers
And of my fathers' fathers –
A thing of the imagination!

But when all my children
Had lice in their heads
All at one time,
This mother
Who they say is my mother's sister,
Said I shouldn't clean their heads
All in one day
Because when it comes to falling sick
They will all fall sick in one day –

All at once!
She said
I should clean Nkeng's head today
Awung's head tomorrow
And Leke's head the other tomorrow;
All this because when in comes to falling sick
They all shouldn't fall sick in one day.
But
This mother
Who is my mother's sister
Is the White God's child.
So,
When I think about
This cleaning of heads
On three different days
Sleep finishes in my head.

III

This mother
Who is my mother's sister
Worships her White God
On different days of the week.

This week,
It is on *asieh* –
The day we speak to our Gods
And give food and drinks
To those beneath the clay.
Yes, on *asieh*
She joins the others
In the house of their White God

To shout like a male goat
Whose testicles are being removed.
They shout and stiffen their bodies
As if they have been attacked by tetanus.
They say
They are shouting praises to their God –
One would think their God is deaf.
One would think their God is an iguana.

Next week
They meet on *alung* –
The day no hoe cuts the soil
Nor machete the bushes –
And shout as if they had never shouted before.

And the other week
They meek on *ankoah* –
The day our Manjong fighters
Remember the god of war –
Not only to shout but to cry
As if their God has lost his brother.

When I asked her,
This woman who is my mother's sister,
Whether they had no fixed day
In our eight-day week
To worship their God
She said the day was *sabat*,
That is was number seven day
Of their seven-day week.
The day their God chose to rest.
He chose to rest

As if he had been splitting fire wood
For six days running.
But,
When I think about this *sabat*
That has no fix day in the week –
This week
It falls on *asieh*
Next week
It falls on *alung*
The other week
It falls on *ankoah* –
For true,
When I think about this *sabat*
That falls on different days of the week
Sleep finishes in my head.

IV

This mother
Who is my mother's sister
Says strange things to me.
She quarrels over my sending my woman
To rest with her parents
Whenever she has a stomach.
She says
My writing books
Is no excuse to stay alone
Especially when my woman
Is carrying a stomach.
She says
A woman who has a stomach
Must continue to sleep with her man.

She says
If you don't sleep with your woman
Now that she has a stomach
How will milk enter her breast?
But
When I try to imagine
What sleeping with a woman
Who has a stomach
Has to do with the milk in her breast
Sleep finishes in my head.

Steve Biko and His Fist

There once lived a man …
He rose to the height of the baobab,
Not to harvest nuts on the tallest palm
But to clear the place of cobwebs.

And do you know what happened to him?

No. Tell us.

Well, it was my father who told me the story
Of this man called Steve Biko.

Who?

Steve Biko,
That was his name.
He once lived in a far away country,
A country they call South Africa.
They say the skins of the people there
Are not like the skins of our bodies.
They say some are as black as the soot
That gather on the bamboo ceilings
Of our mothers' kitchens.
They say some are as white
As the excrement of a sick fowl.
They say some are as red
As the anus of a gorilla.
They say some have patches of skin
Like that of the leopard.
They say some change the look of their skin

As the chameleon does.

What?

They say the house in which they live
Has rooms of different sizes and shapes.
They say they all live in different rooms
And no door opens to the other.
They say they are like children from the same vagina
Living like cats and dogs,
With none able to force a smile from the others.

And this man, Steve Biko,
Gave up father and mother,
Gave up brothers and sisters,
Gave up wife and children,
To throw down and to root out
The walls that divided this house,
The walls that made this house
As divided as the fingers are.

He did?

He did just that,
And did it with a fist;
Clenched those fingers were,
Hard that blow was,
And the chips came falling down
From the walls of that house.

He did?

He did just that, I say,
And the noise from the falling chips
Echoed in the belly of the house
Like the noise from the big water
That echo in the belly of our hills.
That noise filtered through
To everyone's inside
Like rain water entering the belly of the earth.
And sleep began to finish in the heads
Of the people in that house
The way a cracked gourd drains its content.

And they began to come round
As he whose sleep is disturbed
By hooting owls on roof tops.
And when those with skins of soot
Got up from their child-like sleep
Their eyes saw
How the walls that divided them from their brothers were.
And realising at last that they were like caged birds
They all joined to finish the work Steve Biko had started.
They worked to the rhythm of their songs:
Songs of faith,
Songs of hope,
Songs of praise.

Those with white skins,
Those who had divided the house,
Began to realise how choking

The dust from the falling walls was.
But they would not say it was the dust
That was choking them to death.
They said that what was choking them
Was not the dust but the smell from the bodies
Of the people with skins of soot.

What?

They said these people with skins of soot
Smell like the shit of a dog;
That they smell
Like the anus of a cat;
That they smell
Like the urine of a he-goat.
And for this reason
They must stay away.
For this reason
They must stay apart.

What? Apartheid?

That is the name they gave to it.
They had been living apart
Until people started blowing down
The walls that divided them.
Steve Biko's blow echoed in their bellies
And for this a rope was thrown around his neck
As we do to catch a pig.
For this, they flung him into a fence.

What?

Yes, but the fence was not like the ones
In which we put our pigs.
Ours are of sticks stuck into the earth.
That is why our pigs run away.
Steve Biko's fence was made of mounted stones
With edges as sharp as a taper's machete.
The top was covered with thorns of iron,
Thorns as sharp as the teeth of a rat,
Thorns as sharp as the prickles of a porcupine,
Thorns as sharp as the claws of a hawk,
Thorns as sharp as the beak of a vulture.
And so Steve Biko could not run away.
He could not run away from death.
He could not run away from the axe
That chopped off his sense-pass-King head.
He could not run away from the fire
That burnt his tortoise-shell body.

Oooh !

Today,
The flame of that fire
Continues to burn in that country.

Today,
The flame of that fire
Is making the people
See through the fog over the land.

Today,
The flame of that fire

Is helping the anger in the people's belly boil
Like palm oil in a cooking pot.

Today,
The pot is vomiting out oil
On the heads of those
Whose skins are as white
As the excrement of a sick fowl.

This is the story of Steve Biko.
This is the story my father told me.

LEEWAY

My back to the wind
I see rain greening the fields
That will feed our cattle
And give us back our lives.

My back to the wind
I see dead leaves giving birth to corn
That will fill our mothers' barns
And give us back our lives.

My back to the wind
I see dead logs spitting out mushrooms
That will spice our mothers' soup pots
And give us back our lives.

My back to the wind
I see thorny trees producing juice
That will freshen up our throats
And give us back our lives.

My back to the wind
I see the earth laying termites
That will fill our stomachs at tale time
And give us back our lives.

www.ingramcontent.com/pod-product-compliance
Lightning Source LLC
LaVergne TN
LVHW010544100826
845148LV00013B/2595

* 9 7 8 0 6 1 5 8 9 5 8 2 6 *